Cat Massage for Kids
Simple Massage Anyone Can Use to Bond with Their Cats

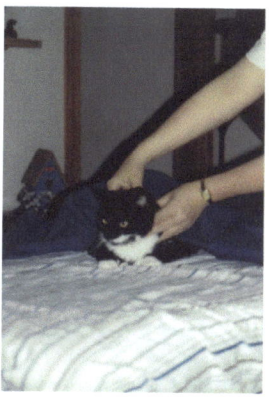

Heidi L. Schlatter

Copyright © 2012 by Heidi L. Schlatter

Freddie Boy Press

Granby, CT

All rights reserved.

ISBN: 978-0-9882673-0-5

DEDICATION

In Loving Memory of my parents, Ethel Dissell Cummings and Charles C. Schlatter

CONTENTS

	Acknowledgments	i
1	Introduction	1
2	Getting a "Read" on Kitty	Pg #5
3	Let's Get Started	Pg #9
4	The Head and Face	Pg #12
5	Checking In	Pg #24
6	"Raking" Your Kitty	Pg #26
7	The Tummy	Pg #32
8	Kids Who Love Their Kitties	Pg #33
9	Finishing Up	Pg #36
10	Final Thoughts	Pg #38

ACKNOWLEDGMENTS

Specisl thanks to the following for pictures they provided:

Roberta Bordanaro for the the Cover Kitty

Jessica Miller for Connor and Molly

Darlene Caldwell for Kelly, Brittany, and Sammy as well as Kelly, AJ, and Sammy

Pudge says, "Meow" ("I'm ready!")

INTRODUCTION

Though I am a licensed massage therapist and can hardly resist writing about medical benefits and technical aspects of massage, my greater intention is to address the simple communication of touch.

I hope this book helps to bond child and cat as well as child and parent. Older children, 8 and up, reading this should be able to understand the information on their own, perform the exercises with their cats, and have the ability to observe the body signals from the animal to determine how well it's being received.

Younger children would do well to have a mom, dad, or older sibling present to demonstrate and supervise the interaction between their child and the cat to ensure that the experience goes in a positive fashion for both. This process can serve to teach children the proper and kind way to approach an animal as well as what gentle touch and kind intention can do to help form a strong bond between human and animal.

Likewise, any adults wanting to make use of simple massage to strengthen their bond with their cat – this might fit the bill without having to worry about anatomy and feeling tight areas on your cat, etc. These are some of the methods I have found to help with my rescue kitties to develop trust as well as a strong bond with me. I've shared some of these techniques with those who have cats with a bit of aggressive, rough behavior, and have been pleased to hear of the transformations they have witnessed.

The Cover Kitty, Shana, was a great little rescue kitty who never was very trusting of people and pretty much secluded herself to the upstairs portion of their home. I would go to the house weekly to do massage on Roberta, Shana's pet mama, and over a period of time whenever the massage table was being set up Shana would come downstairs looking for her own session! It was the cutest thing! I had been warned not to pet her for any length of time or I might experience the consequences of her double-pawed set of claws so I respected those limits. I know it's because I did, that Shana started to seek out my non-threatening touch each week and welcomed it for longer periods as the weeks passed.

The picture on the front cover of this book was from the day she surprised us both by jumping onto the table. I lifted the top sheet and she climbed under it and turned around into the position you see her in. She clearly was waiting for her massage session!

Roberta's current rescue kitty, Freshie, who also was never socialized well with humans, has similarly looked forward to my arrival for her weekly massages, jumped on the table and relished every moment of her sessions experiencing kind, gentle touch.

I thought for awhile – I'm a cat whisperer! Well, not quite, but I do understand much of the "thinking" of animals just as anyone can.

Roberta started using some of the strokes mentioned in this book and has noticed Freshie coming around more frequently and sitting closer to her. We're hoping it will eventually encourage Freshie enough to actually sit on her lap at some point.

My most recent example is of a co-worker who pet sits for a rather rough kitty in her neighborhood. This is one of those cats that had learned to play rough and will attack and bite people like they are pretend prey. She started very simply with the strokes on the top of the head for brief sessions. She noticed a difference nearly right away in that the cat approached her and jumped up on her lap! That was not typical as noted by his pet-parents as well. She's going to see how much it might change his aggressive play over a period of time.

I know from first-hand experience that with a calm, patient, and gentle approach, cats can learn to trust and develop very strong bonds with us.

I also feel that the lesson learned by children in considering the feelings of an animal and respecting what or who that animal is, that it is likely to transfer over to the consideration of fellow humans as well. What better way to learn empathy than to learn to think of how an animal who can't speak for himself might feel!

2 GETTING A "READ" ON KITTY

As any cat parent knows, cats can be absolute angels or they can create the most frustrating encounter one could imagine. Cats call the shots in most aspects of life with them, and oddly enough, we humans tend to comply without question!

When it comes to physically interacting with your kitty, and even thinking about offering massage to him, you really need to tune in to what he's feeling at any given moment and what his energy level is. Nobody is going to benefit from trying to force a massage session, and ultimately it would be quite counterproductive. He'll end up stressed and possibly a little mistrusting of your intentions. And you'll end up wondering why you even bothered to try to bond with that ungrateful so-and-so!

Cats you've raised from kittens are going to be a lot easier to approach provided you've always handled them a lot. Cats adopted into your home as adults possibly from rescue organizations might be a bit more of a challenge, but stand to benefit the most from this process. It will indeed be worth your while to take time with this because it develops a strong trust between you and your kitty. And the relaxation resulting from the session will be savored by you both!

Even the most laid back "couch potato" kitty can become very contrary when their human decides they should like something. Often if the process of introducing massage is undertaken in a gradual manner, even a more contrary type can learn to look forward to his massage sessions. They may even seek you out to receive one!

Hopefully, your cat is already ok about sitting near you, or on your lap, and likes being petted. You want the cat at ease and ideally in one of *his* favorite spots. It's ok if he's sitting, lying down, or even standing, as long as he's wanting to be there. You don't want to make him endure anything he's not happy and relaxed with throughout the session.

Relaxed Merlin

With children under 4 years old, the concentration should be to do the basic stroking of the kitty in a gentle fashion, and mom or dad should be there to demonstrate it for them perhaps even guiding the child's hand. Little tykes tend to not realize their own strength and certainly don't fully understand what they can inflict upon others. I've seen too often when children are permitted to carry a kitty with arm slung around the neck, or by one leg with kitty dangling, or even dragging them by the tail. These actions are really unkind and if the child is not old enough to understand the proper way to treat the cat, then he or she needs to be kept from such interactions with the animal until they do. (Too often, when the animal turns to defend itself – it is deemed the fault of the animal and they are sent to a shelter or even put down, especially when involving dogs.)

It's my bet that those who are reading this book are not of that mindset and are likely to be the adopters of rescued animals interested in promoting their well-being.

The bottom line is that you want your kitties and other fur-babies to enjoy the company of your children and absolutely trust them. As each child matures and gains understanding of these principles, they can be taught more about other strokes to use to further attract their kitty!

My suggestion for guiding your small child is to have them first try applying what you are teaching them on your own leg or arm. The shin would serve well as the spine of the kitty and as the spine is an area easily injured by excessive force, you want to be sure they are not pressing hard or pinching this area. You, the parent, can see if your child understands what you are teaching in this manner.

3 LET'S GET STARTED!

The best strokes to use to start are what we do naturally - long sweeping strokes with our whole hand from head to tail a few times.

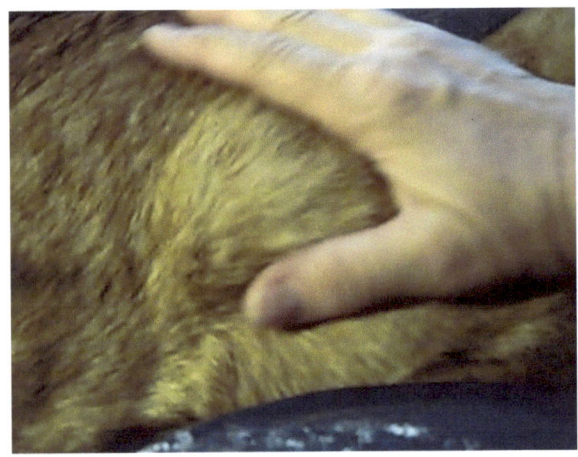

Try to keep your hand open and relaxed as it follows the contours of the cat's body. There is no need to apply any real pressure while doing this, but if your cat is one that clearly likes this type of "petting" then you can add a little pressure. Glide up the tail barely touching it.

This can serve as your greeting to kitty and then you'll want to proceed to the "hook" by working around the head and neck. Most kitties can't resist having someone scratch them behind the ears a bit. And most of these strokes should be greatly enjoyed by your cat.

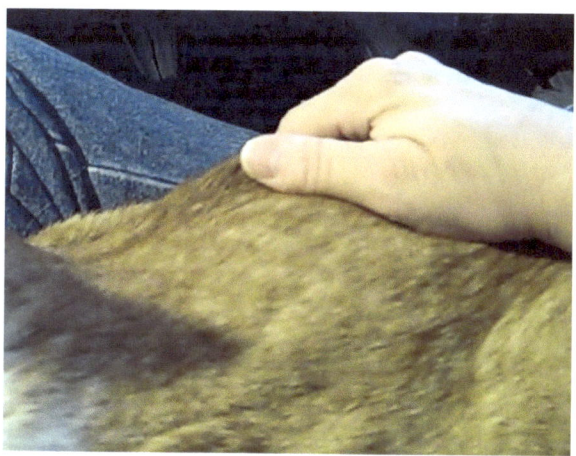

Above, over the spine area I like to cup my hand a bit to not be making contact with any of the vertebrae as it really doesn't appeal much to a cat to have skin pushed against bone.

Below, try tracing with your fingers on both sides of the spine with no real pressure. Many cats like that. Pudge is a little ticklish when I do this, but he doesn't seem to mind.

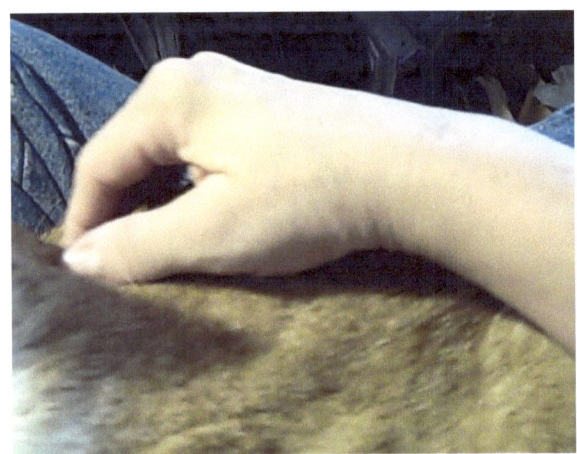

4 THE HEAD AND FACE

I've found that many cats are more receptive to other areas of their bodies being touched after you relax them by working their head, neck, face, and ears. So after the long body sweeps, I would suggest you move up to the head area.

Your cat is going to react differently the first few times you do this, but will quickly learn that he really enjoys it, and he'll likely welcome future sessions.

Now, relax your hand and just rub lightly over the nose and then a little firmer on the top of their head and down to the base of the neck. Watch the cat's body language as you go. If he is pulling away or really starting with tail movement, try a different stroke, scratch behind his ears, or even stop for a bit.

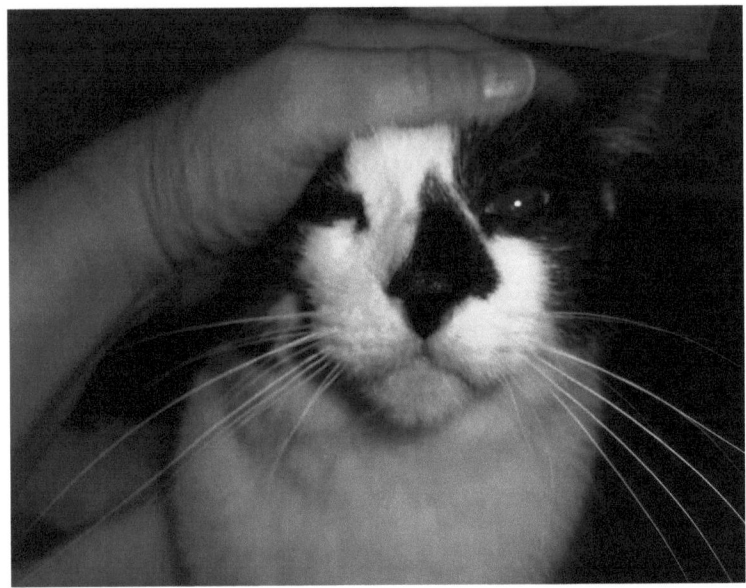

Merlin, pictured above, sometimes wonders what I am up to at first, but soon appreciates the way it feels.

As you repeat that, open your thumb to drop down along the side of the mouth, over the cheek, and along the side of the neck. Be sure to include those areas on the other side of his face and neck as well.

The head and face strokes are something many cats would let you do all day long, so I add a little extra time for those. The described sweeping strokes are great introductory strokes that go a little further than just petting a cat's head.

Something I found to be very effective with my less tame kitty, and others have reported it to work nicely with their non-socialized kitties, is a stroke where I try to duplicate the feeling of a caring kitty washing the face of another, like their mommies used to do. The easiest is to use your thumb and do short strokes above the eyebrow area toward the top of the head. Relax the thumb and try to use very light pressure as you do several small strokes working your way across the entire top of the head. It's not clear in the following photo, but I am making contact with just the thumb pad.

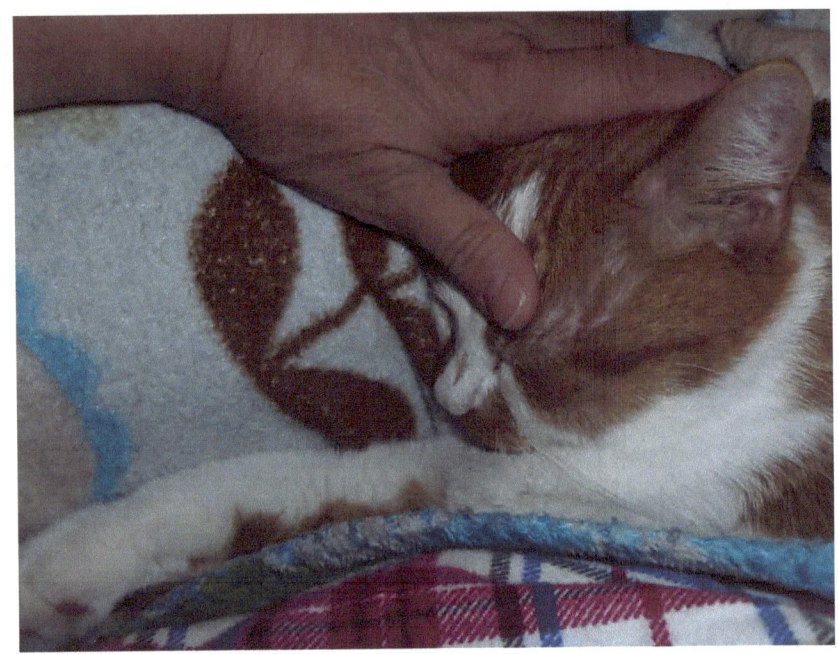

Repeat strokes over same area a few times and then move over a bit.

Use no pressure to brush over the eye and up onto the forehead.

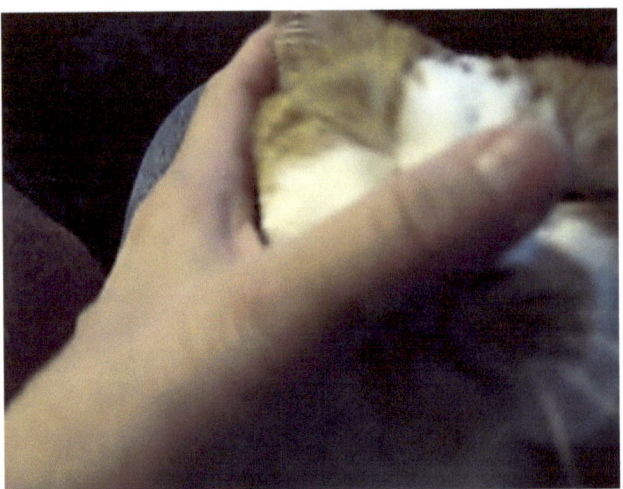

Above, I adjusted my hand position down lower on his head and continued to use the thumb and the hinging action to include from the side of the nose – up along the cheek area.

And below, you have to include along the side of the mouth as most cats love this area rubbed to aid their mission in marking everything! At the corner of the mouth and up you can put a bit of pressure continuing toward the ear - not too hard though. Many times you just have to hold your thumb there and kitty will complete the stroke themselves!

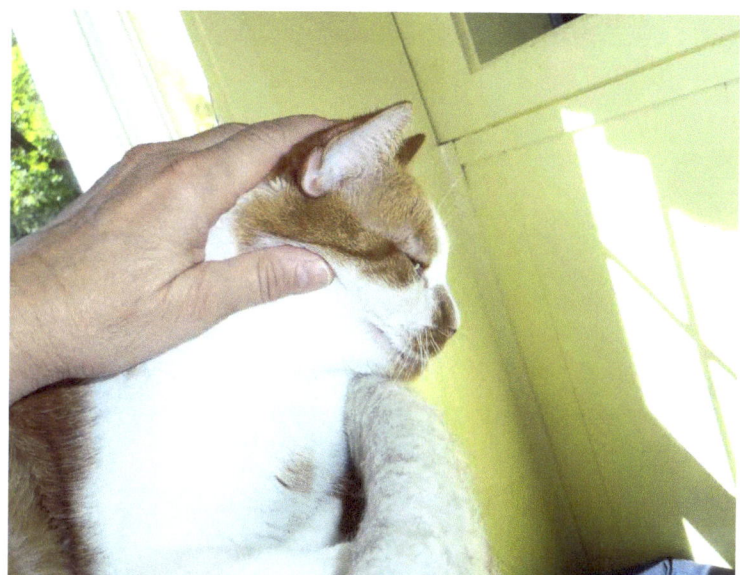

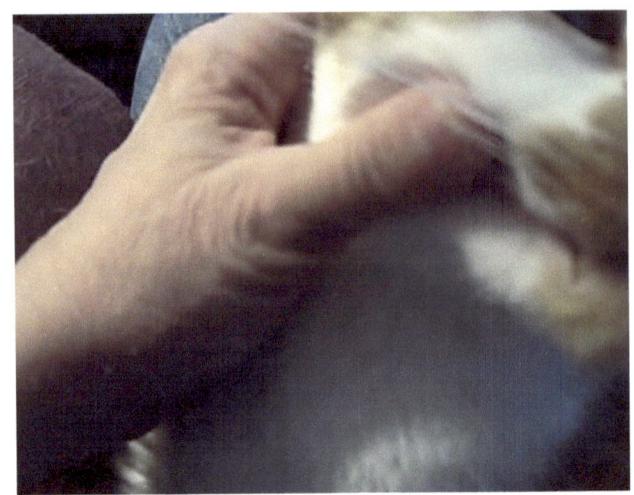

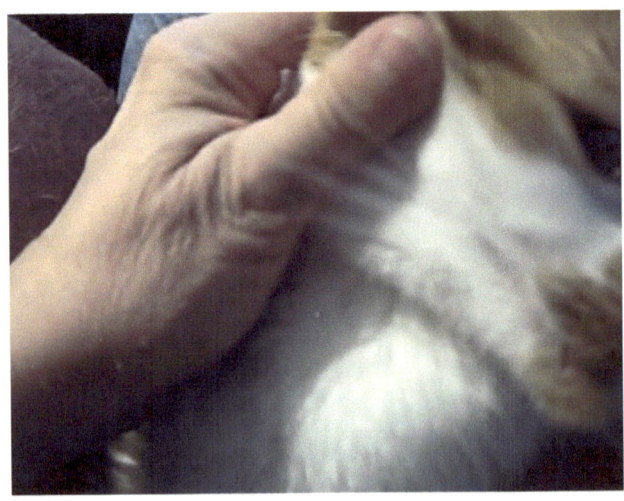

Repeat this stroke a few times and then it's easy to move right up to the ear.

Remember, you never-ever-ever need to put your fingers into the ear canal as you could cause discomfort and possible damage by doing so. You're just going to work on the ear flap from tip to base where it attaches to the head.

Hold the ear between thumb and forefinger and do small circles with no pressure. Move up and down the entire flap area slowly and gently. Most cats really like this. But remember, anything they are not used to, they might not want done. Each session, try again.

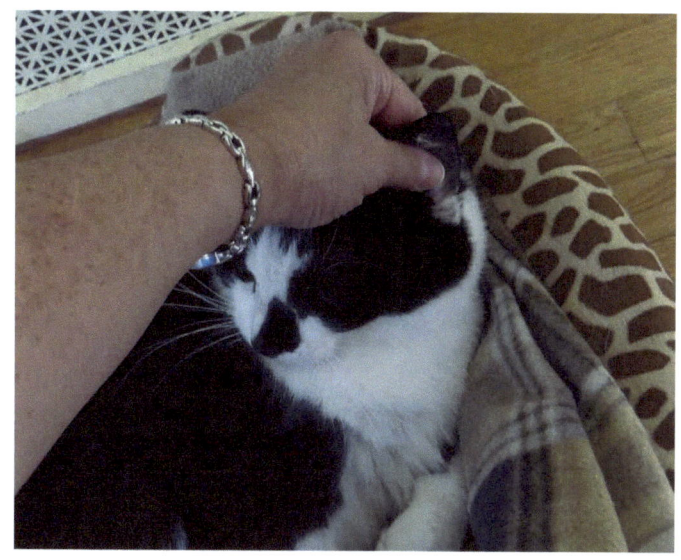

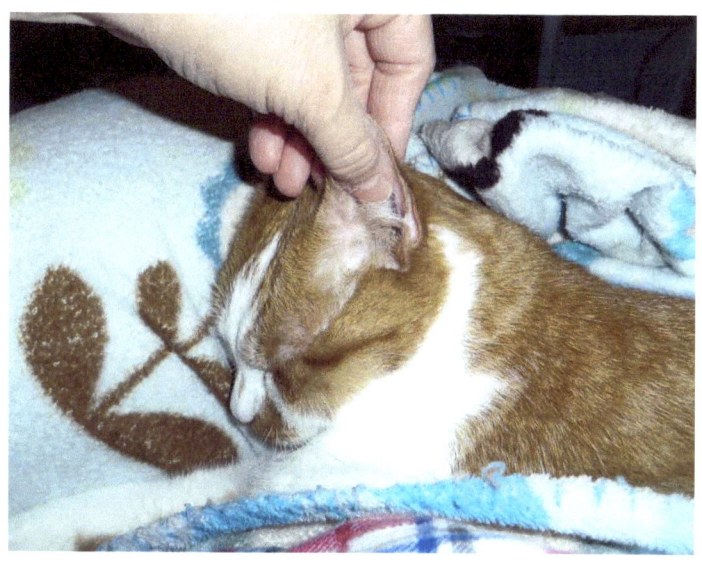

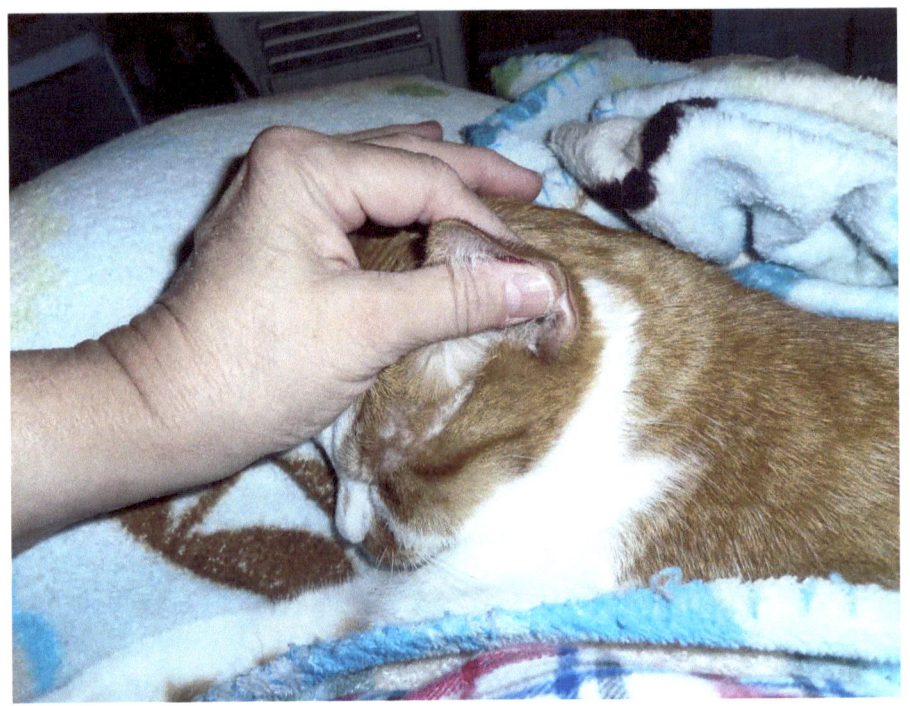

5 CHECKING IN

Along the way you'll want to keep watching how your kitty reacts. Notice what they truly love and what they don't care so much for and whenever they get a little restless, always try to return to those favorite strokes to keep them interested.

A cat getting a bit impatient or even annoyed will often start swinging or thumping their tail. Some will flatten their ears back a little and actually start to look quite grumpy! Ideally, you will be able to identify their restlessness before the grumpy stage and end the session. It's always better if you offer them the option to leave rather than wait until they decide they need to escape.

When starting out with a cat that isn't sure of the whole process of having humans touch them, find the one thing that you know they are comfortable with, spend a couple of minutes doing it, and then tell kitty - "Ok, all done." - while removing your hands altogether. It gives them the option to move away if they desire, and they don't feel forced into it. Odds are after a few times, you'll find they linger longer and welcome more strokes.

If my kitties are being patient, which they generally are with our sessions now, I then will move to various parts of the neck. Lightly rub down the back of the neck, under the chin, avoiding the voice box, and along the sides of the neck too. I bend my fingers and "rake" them through the fur. Use long gentle strokes and even a little extra scratch behind the ears or under the chin.

Verbally reinforce good behavior of your cat. Tell them they are a very good kitty, and you can offer them a treat at the end of a session if you'd like. Fair warning though, is to not have the treat nearby or that's all kitty will be thinking of - finding where that great aroma is coming from!

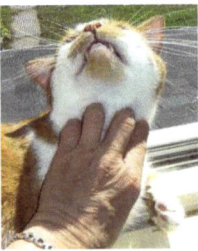

6 "RAKING" YOUR KITTY

They especially like the raking technique applied up the back of the neck, with a light pressure, for several passes to cover the entire area, and then finish by smoothing the fur back down. You can also rake the sides of the neck with and against the fur – always smoothing afterwards. And many kitties also love it when I rake the area between the front legs to the chest using a light pressure.

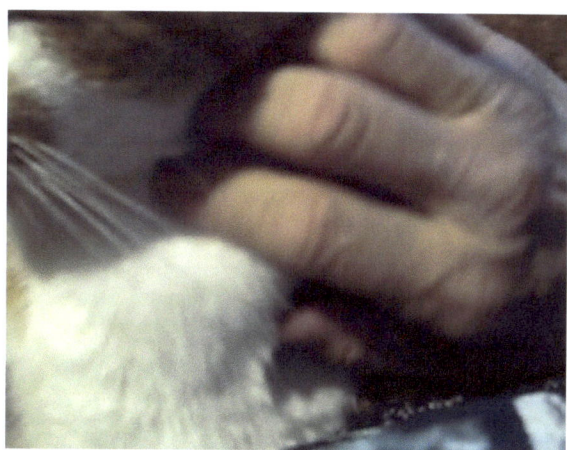

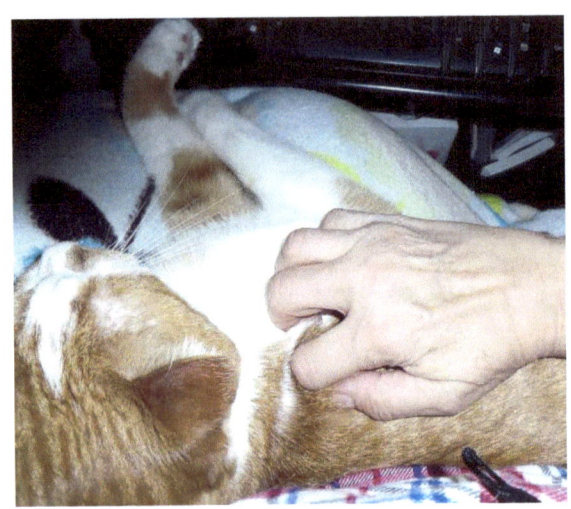

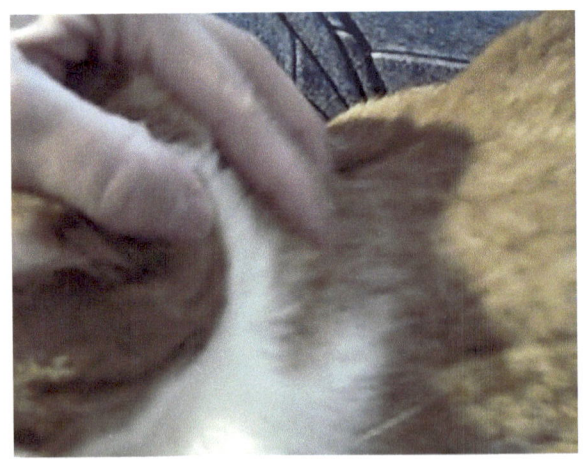

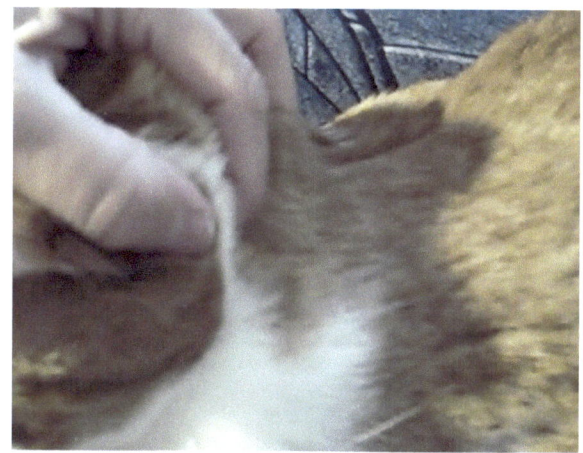

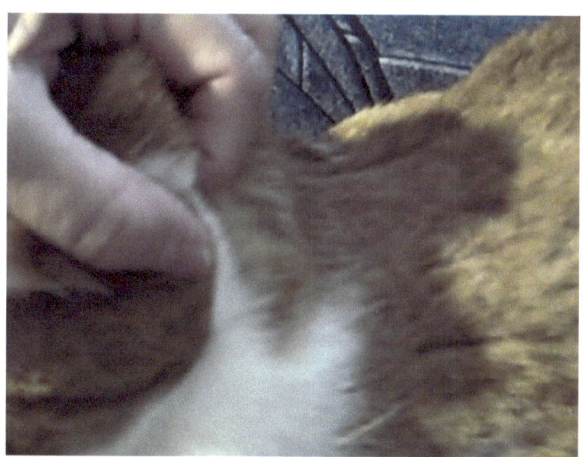

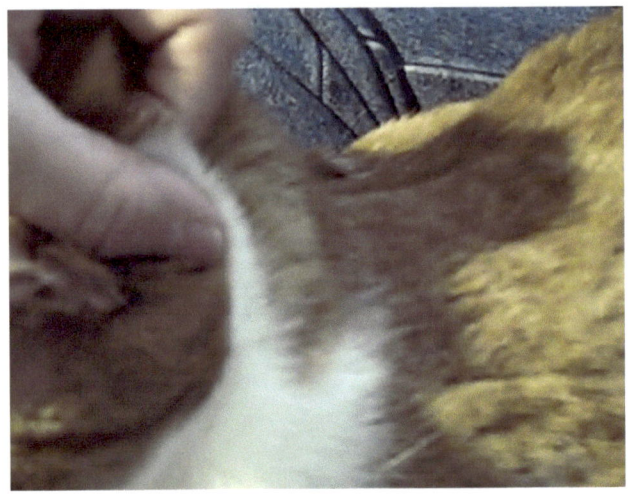

Pudge has a thick coat so my fingers are mostly gliding through fur in these pictures, but I am putting light pressure against the neck. I'm not digging into the tissue, but adding a little firmness to my strokes.

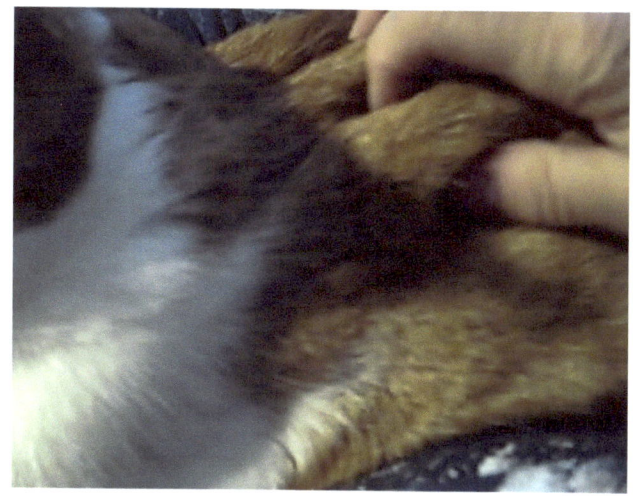

I'm not pinching tissue in these pictures as it sometimes looks. Again, it's his thick coat I'm settling my fingers into. Kitties aren't real fond of you pinching anything.

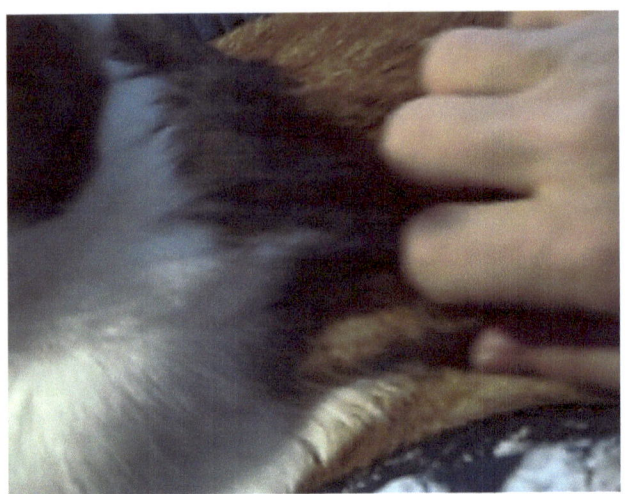

Finger raking can be used all over their body according to what they will tolerate. It massages the muscles nicely and is easiest to do by simply following the direction of hair growth.

7 THE TUMMY

I did not include the belly in this book, as these techniques are intended to soothe your kitty while building trust. For many cats, rubbing their tummies triggers a "wrestling" or fight mode and leads to biting and scratching.

I've met many people who talk of the vicious cat who grabs their arms or legs and bites and scratches them terribly. After further discussion, it's often revealed that someone in the household has "played" with the cat in a rough manner by holding them down on their back and engaging in "play wrestling".

The cat's mind really doesn't know how to split the difference. If your hand is fair game, then so are the ankles, feet, legs, and arms whenever it feels like such an encounter. You just become big prey to them! Just observe the way two cats play and wrestle together. It's what they know and it's best not to encourage that type of relationship with their human family members.

8 KIDS WHO LOVE THEIR KITTIES

This is 2-1/2 year old Connor shown above holding his foster kitty, Molly, very nicely. His parents have taught him to respect animals and always be kind to them. He loves his furry gang and they love him!

Kelly (10 yrs old) is showing her sister, Brittany (5 yrs old), how to gently massage big Sammy. Sammy seems to be enjoying it.

Now it is brother AJ's (4 yrs old) turn to pet Sammy.

Guiding a child's hand is more for toddler ages as they don't understand verbal instructions very well yet. The children with Sammy have all been taught from an early age to be gentle and kind with animals.

9 FINISHING UP

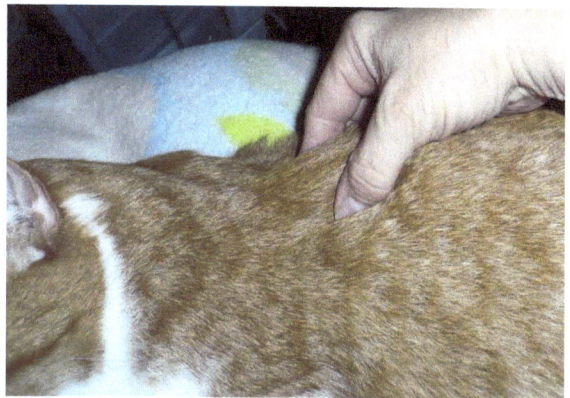

I again run my fingers and thumb along the length of the spine a few times and continue along down the rear legs gently cupping the lower leg down to the paw in my hand. I like to touch the paws and toes as part of a session because many kitties don't like it due to their dislike of having their nails clipped. I even pull a bit on each claw with my own nail. This way they learn nothing terrible happens to them and it could make them a little less contrary when you do want to trim nails. If they clearly dislike this – it's not necessary.

I also cup my hand around their front legs and gently glide down to the paws several times. Many try to pull their feet away from you so just do so to their tolerance level. It might increase over time as they learn that these massage sessions are not something to fear at all.

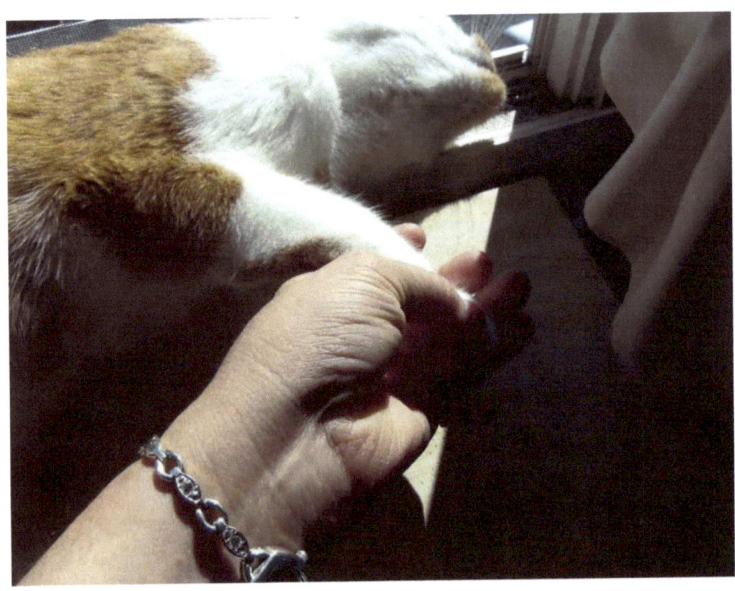

10 FINAL THOUGHTS

Much of the previous massage session is best practiced by older children or adults because it's important not to be forceful at any time throughout the sessions with your cat.

I do think, however, that there are many things that can be shared and taught to younger children proportionate to their age and coordination to enable them to fulfill their innate attraction and love for animals. It's heartwarming to see a kitty run up to their little human seeking attention rather than looking for a place to hide or actually attacking them!

I hope this book will help you practice simple ways to positively affect your relationship with your cat as well as helping to teach your children the correct way to treat a kitty in a gentle and kind fashion. It can only help to produce a healthier happier cat mentally and physically as well. (Even though I didn't concentrate on therapeutic massage techniques, the strokes used in this book can still have a healthy effect on your cat's body and stress levels.)

To you older readers, 8 and up, I hope you enjoy the sessions with your cat and that you'll take what you learn here, and share it with other family members and other kitty families.

Animals deserve our respect and kind treatment. They are not part of our planet to put up with things we humans impose upon them.

Please join me in my dream to make enough of a difference for animals that the next generation of adults will have no need for rescue organizations.

Please be kind to animals!

"Purrrrrr"

ABOUT THE AUTHOR

Heidi Schlatter is the author of *Merlin, The Cat Who Thought He Wasn't,* the first book in the Rescued Animal Tails series. The series of books tell the stories of real rescued animals that have been adopted into their forever homes.

Ms Schlatter has adopted many stray or rescued animals herself, and witnessed many behaviors these animals display because of their questionable beginnings in life. She felt the need to approach the situation from a preventative approach rather than to address the problems later in the life of the animal - whether it's an adult cat new to a household or a kitten that needs to learn how to bond in a positive way with their human family. Mostly, she has seen a need for people to learn to empathize with animals and treat them with respect and kindness.

www.ingramcontent.com/pod-product-compliance
Lightning Source LLC
Chambersburg PA
CBHW042123040426
42450CB00002B/48